WHORE SERIES

Amusing Swear Words To Color

For Stress Releasing

By

Queenie McJody

Happy Coloring!

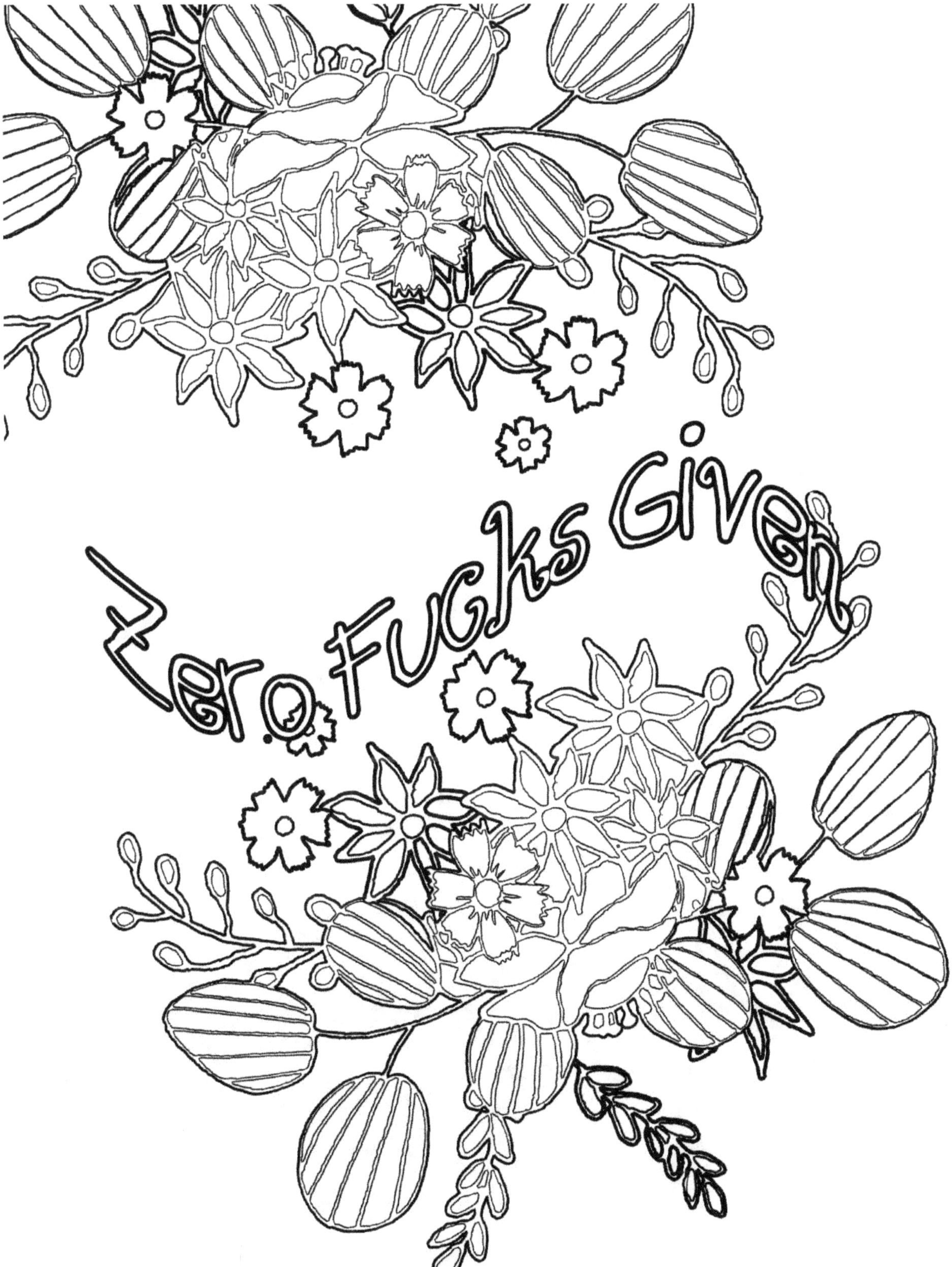
Zero Fucks Given

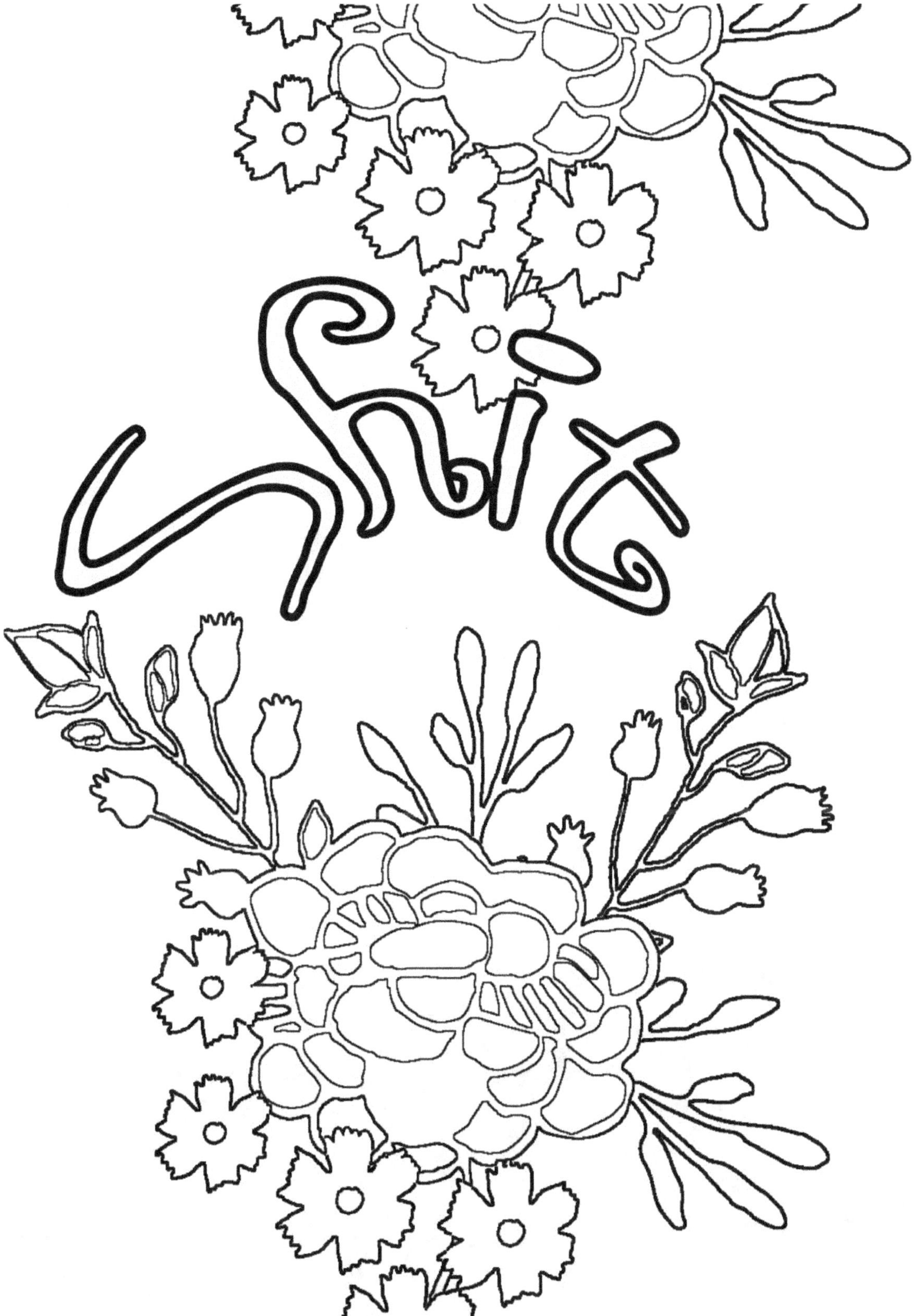
Shit

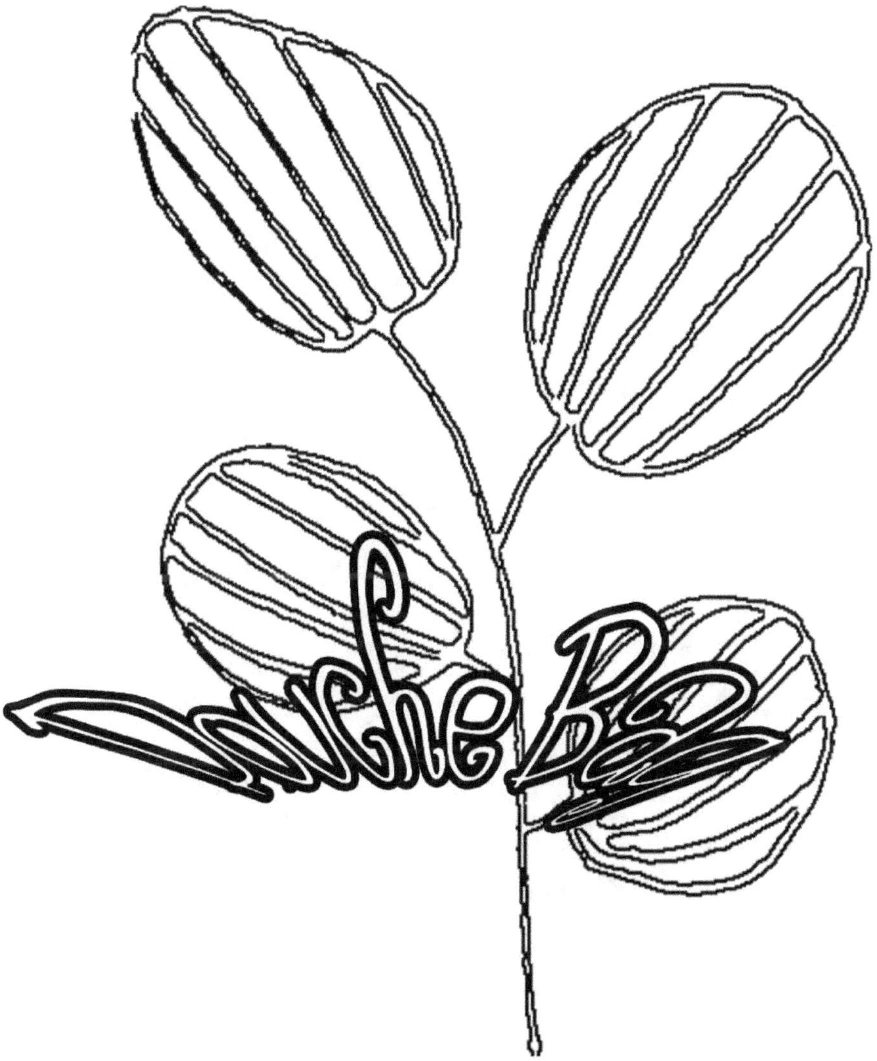

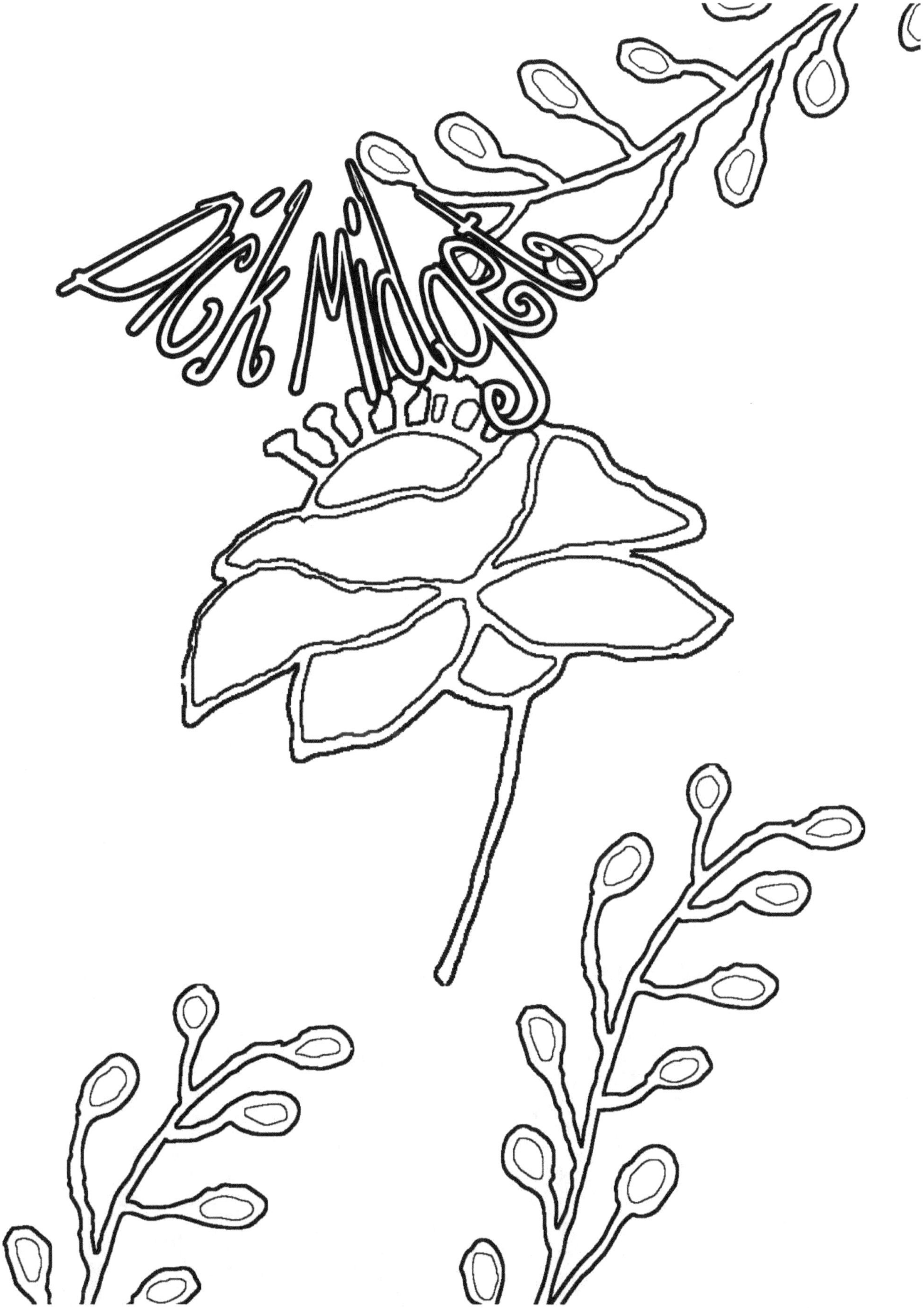

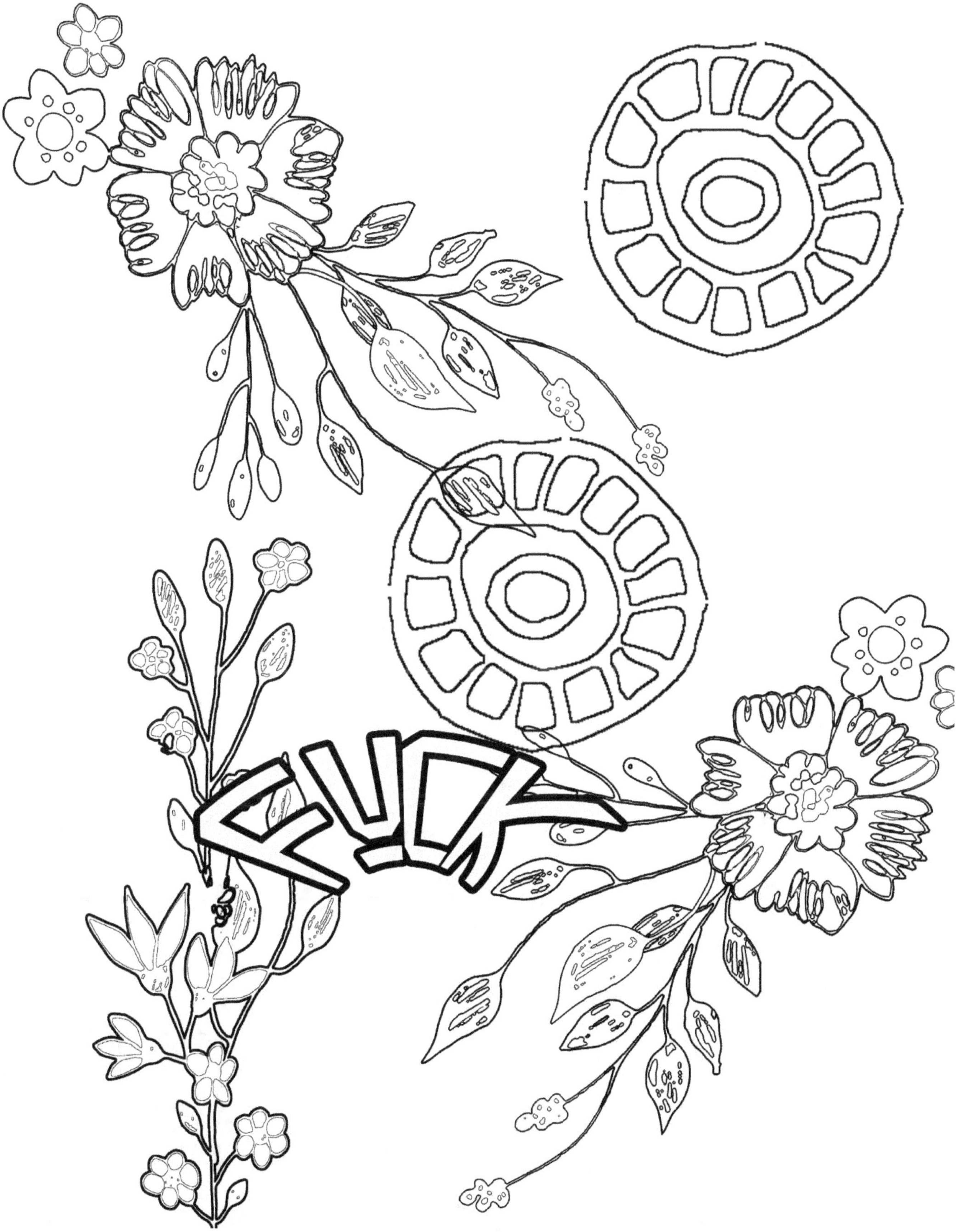
FUCK

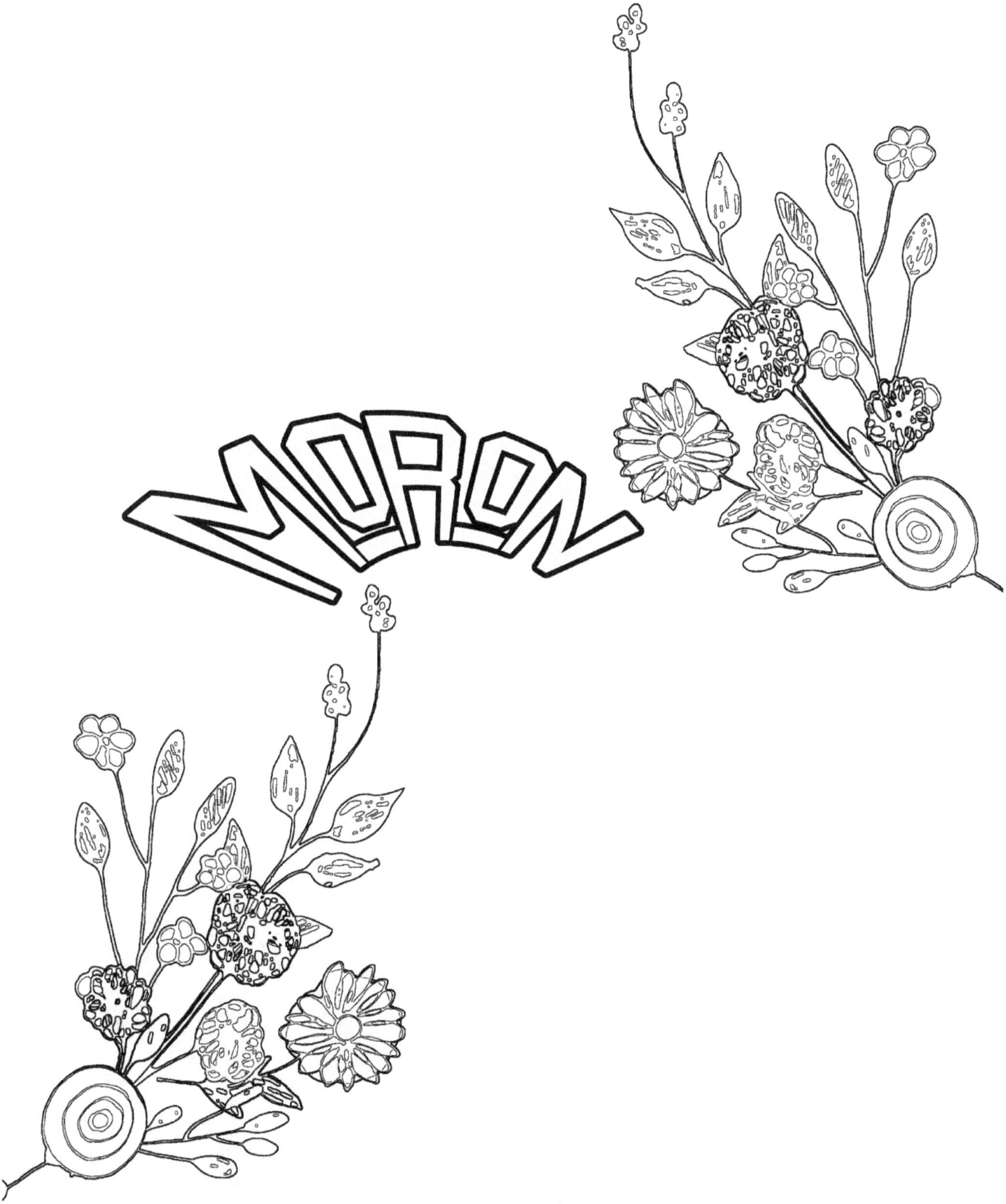
MORON

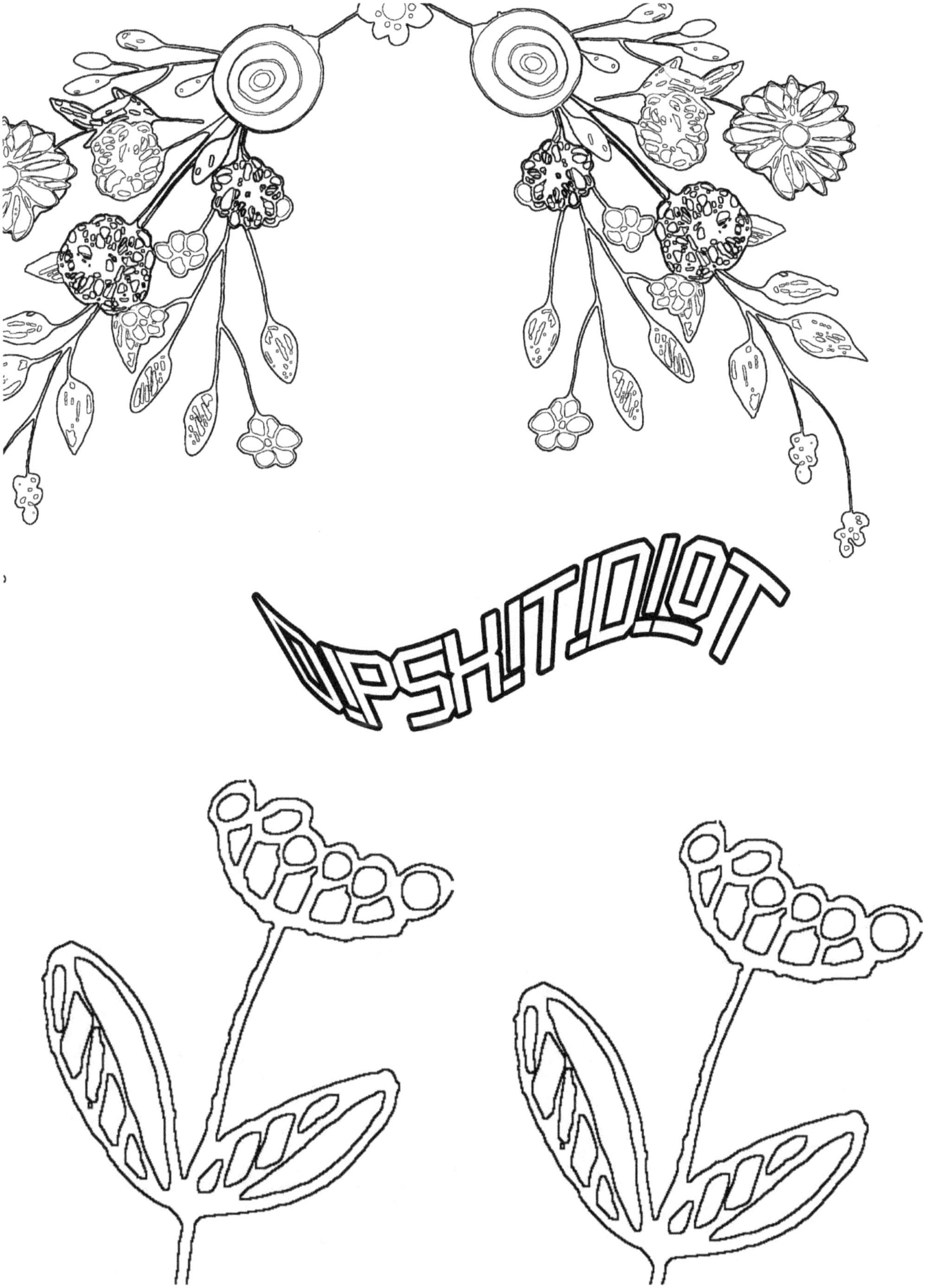
DIPSHITIDIOT

D!PSH!T !D!OT

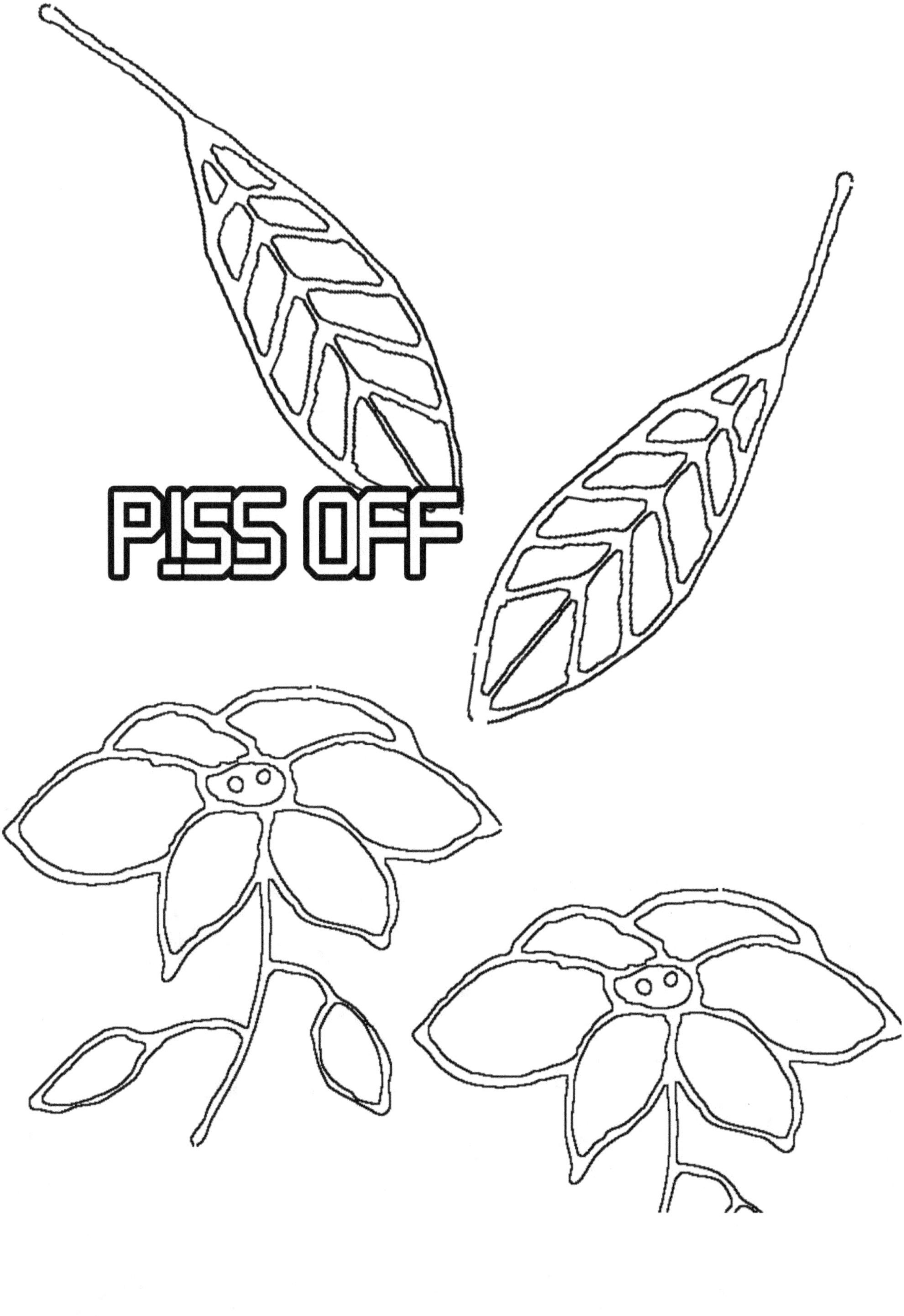
PISS OFF

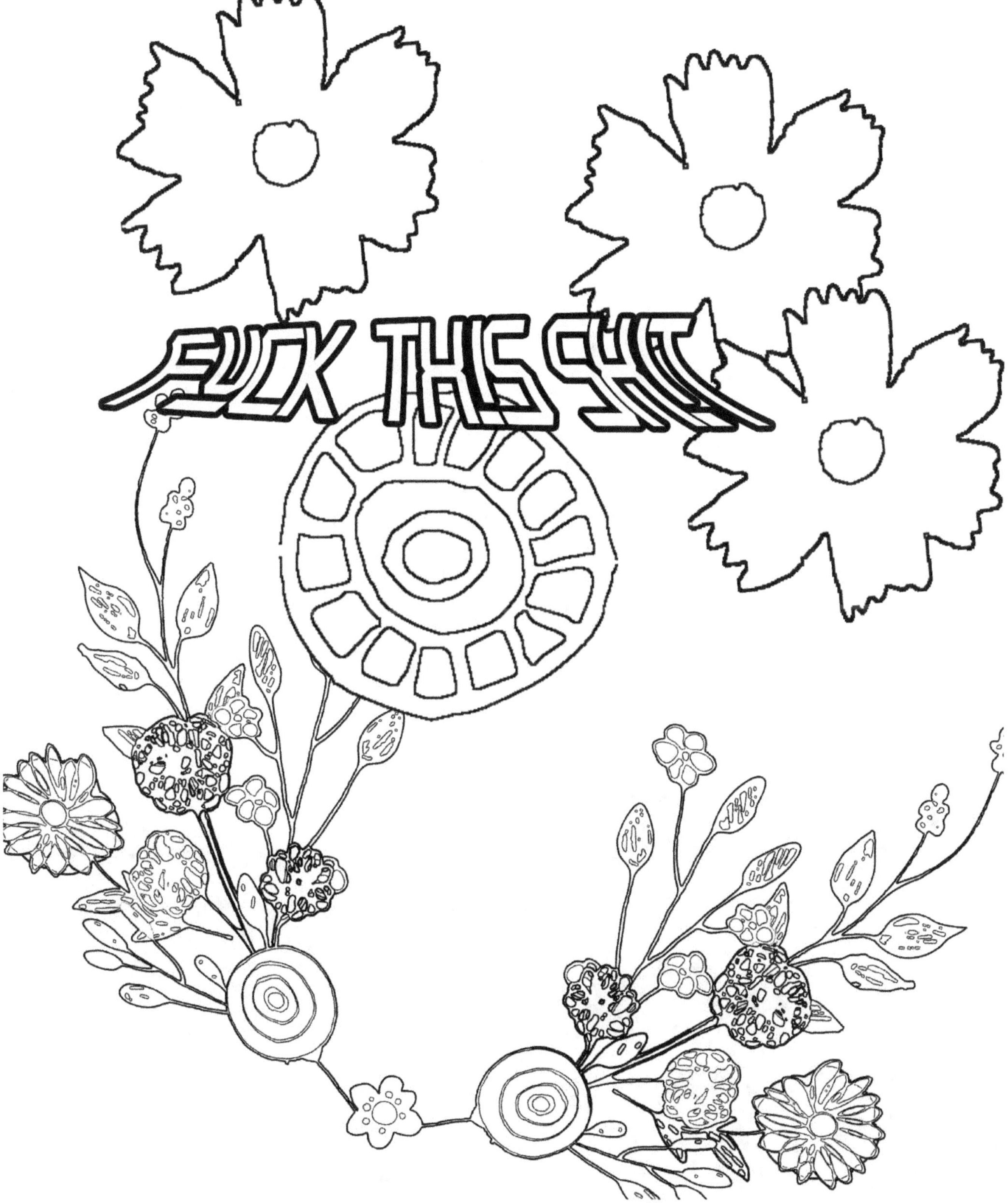
FUCK THIS SHIT

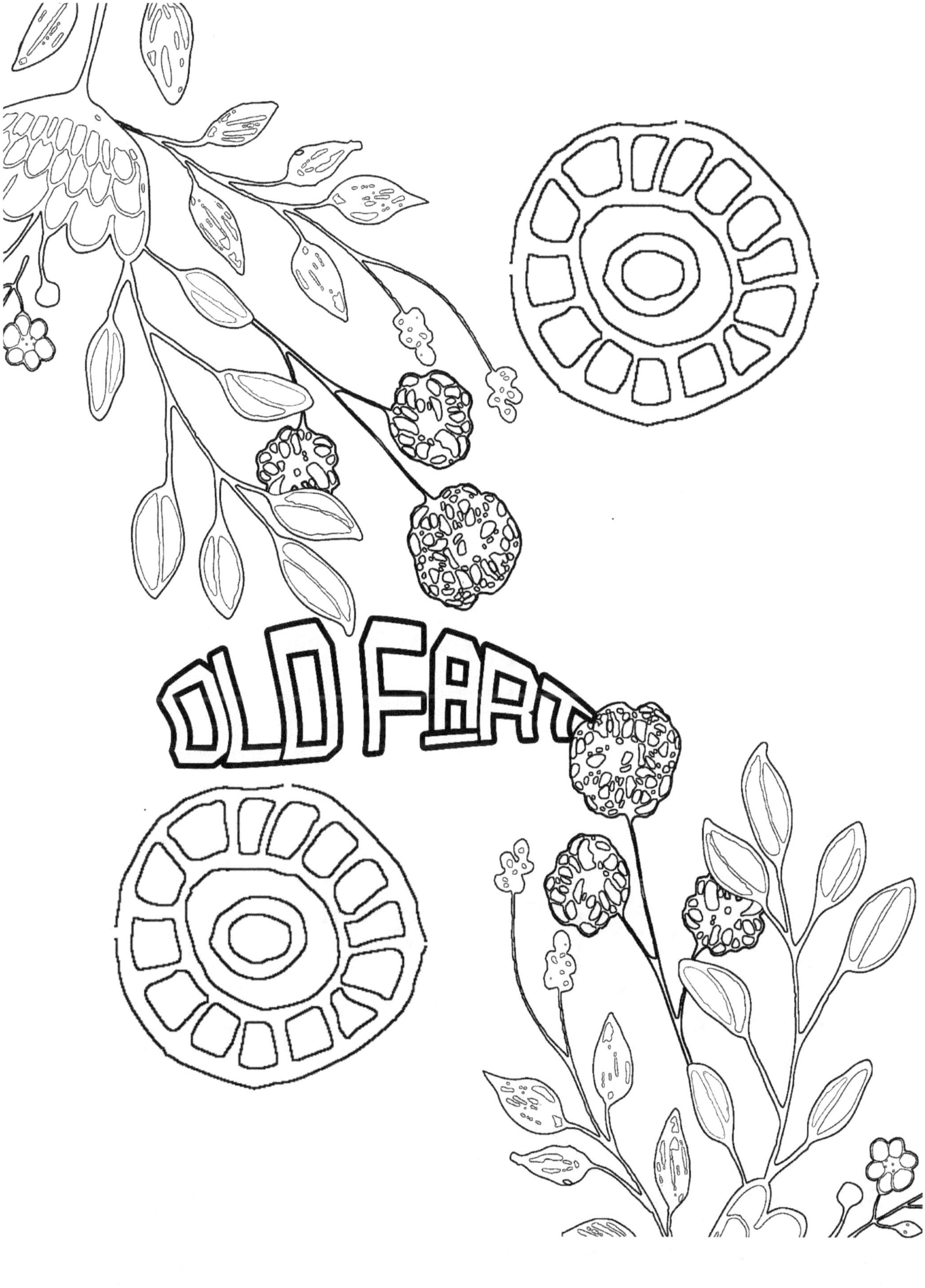
OLD FART

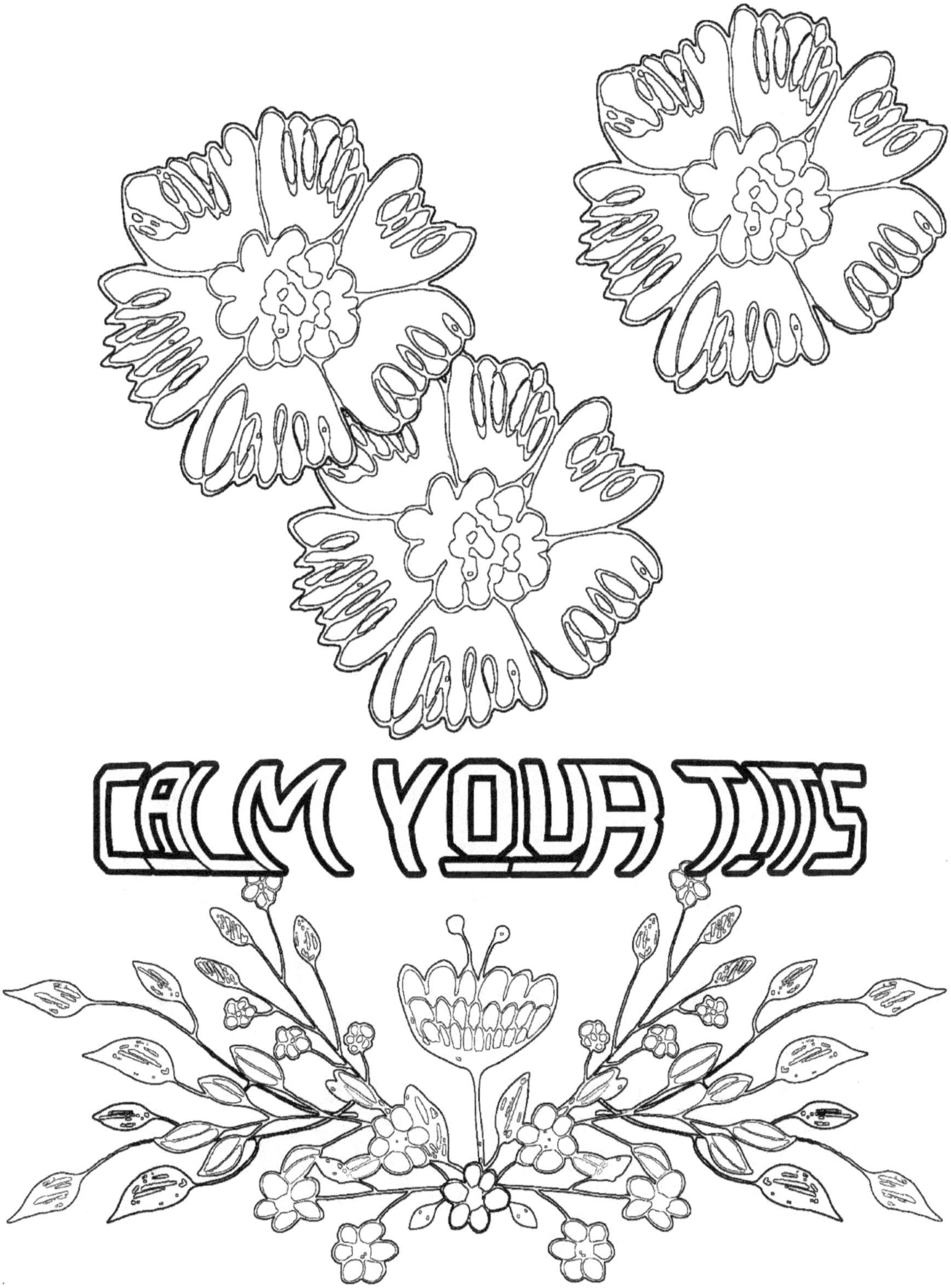
CALM YOUR TITS

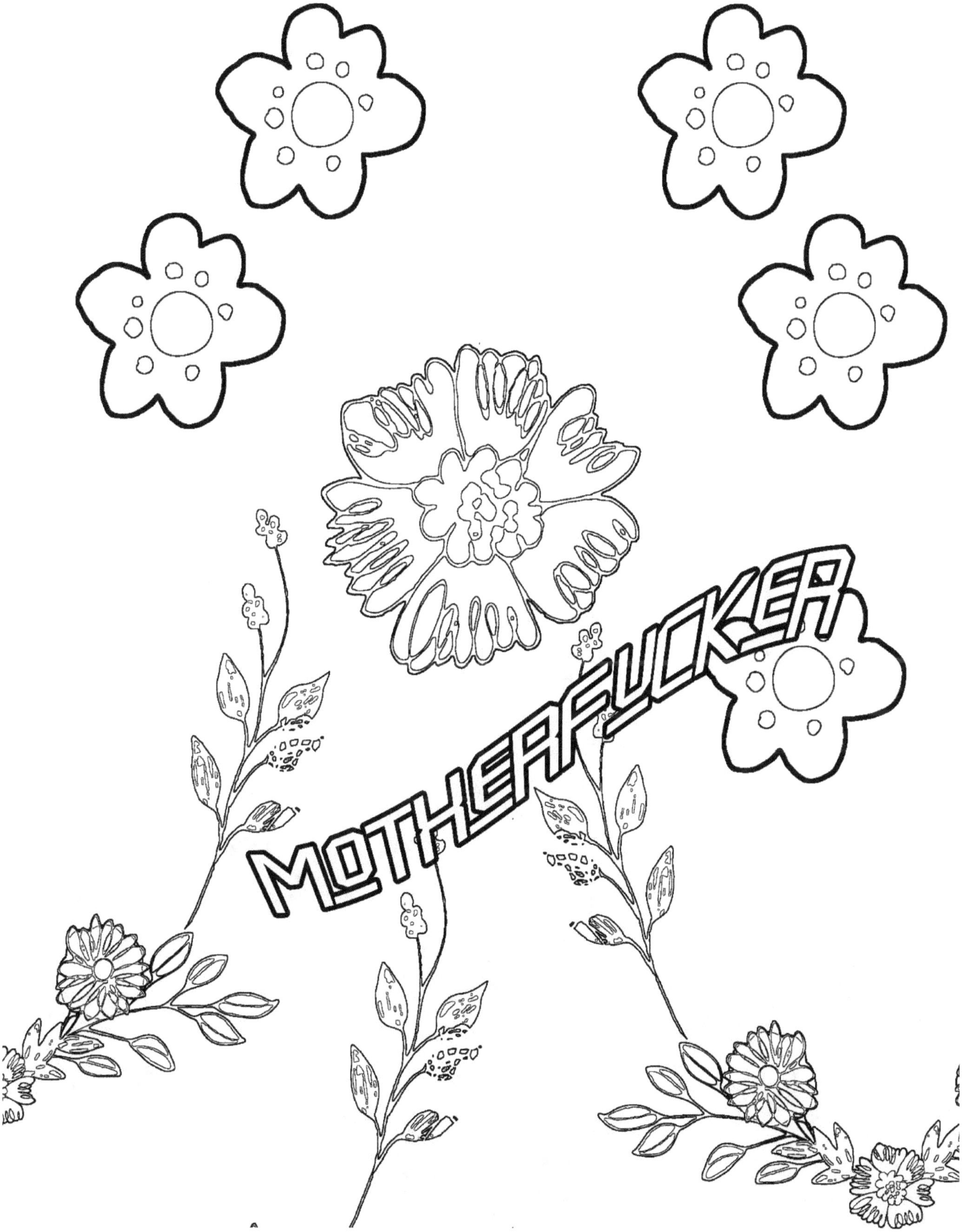
MOTHERFUCKER

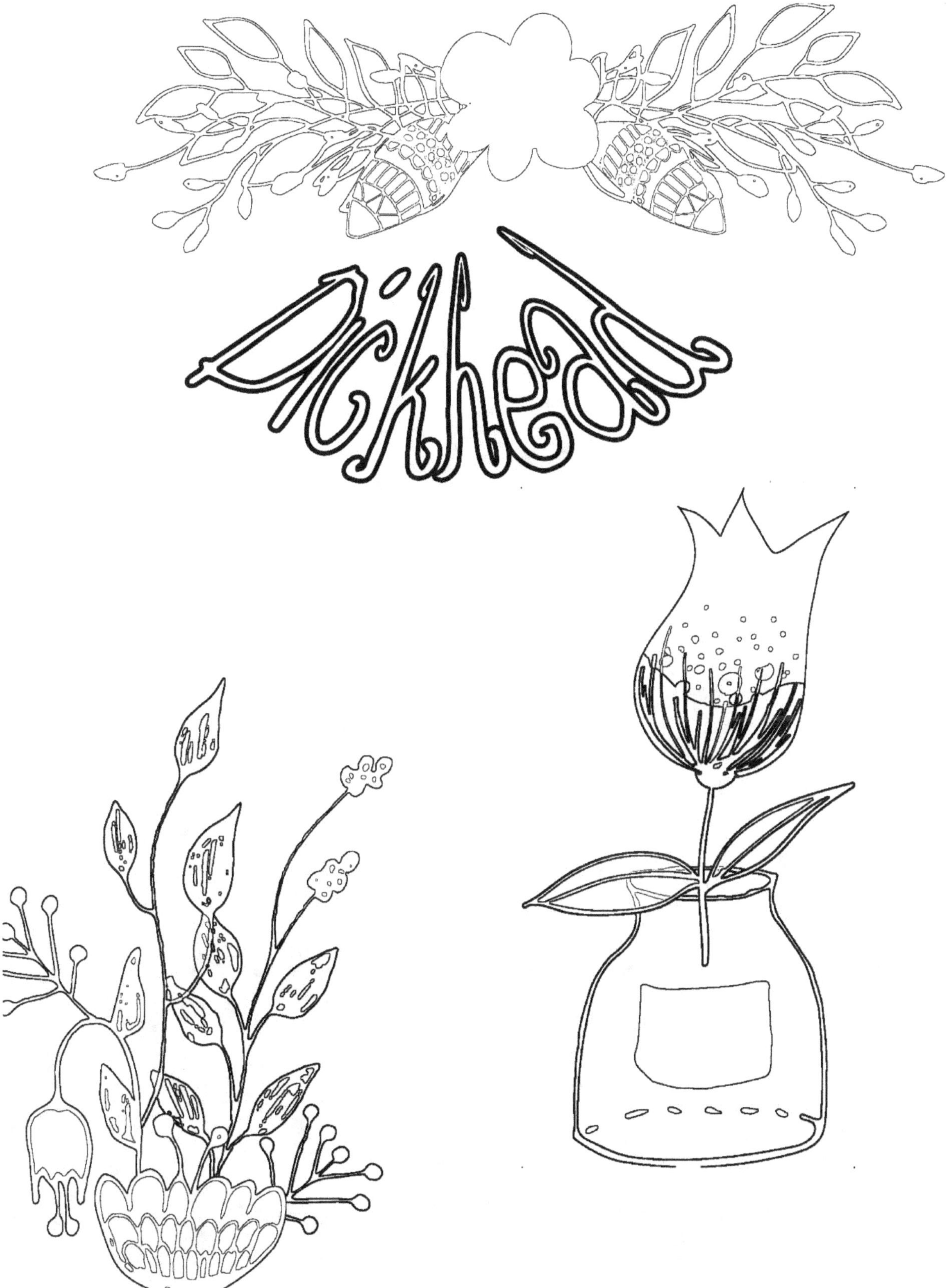
Dickhead

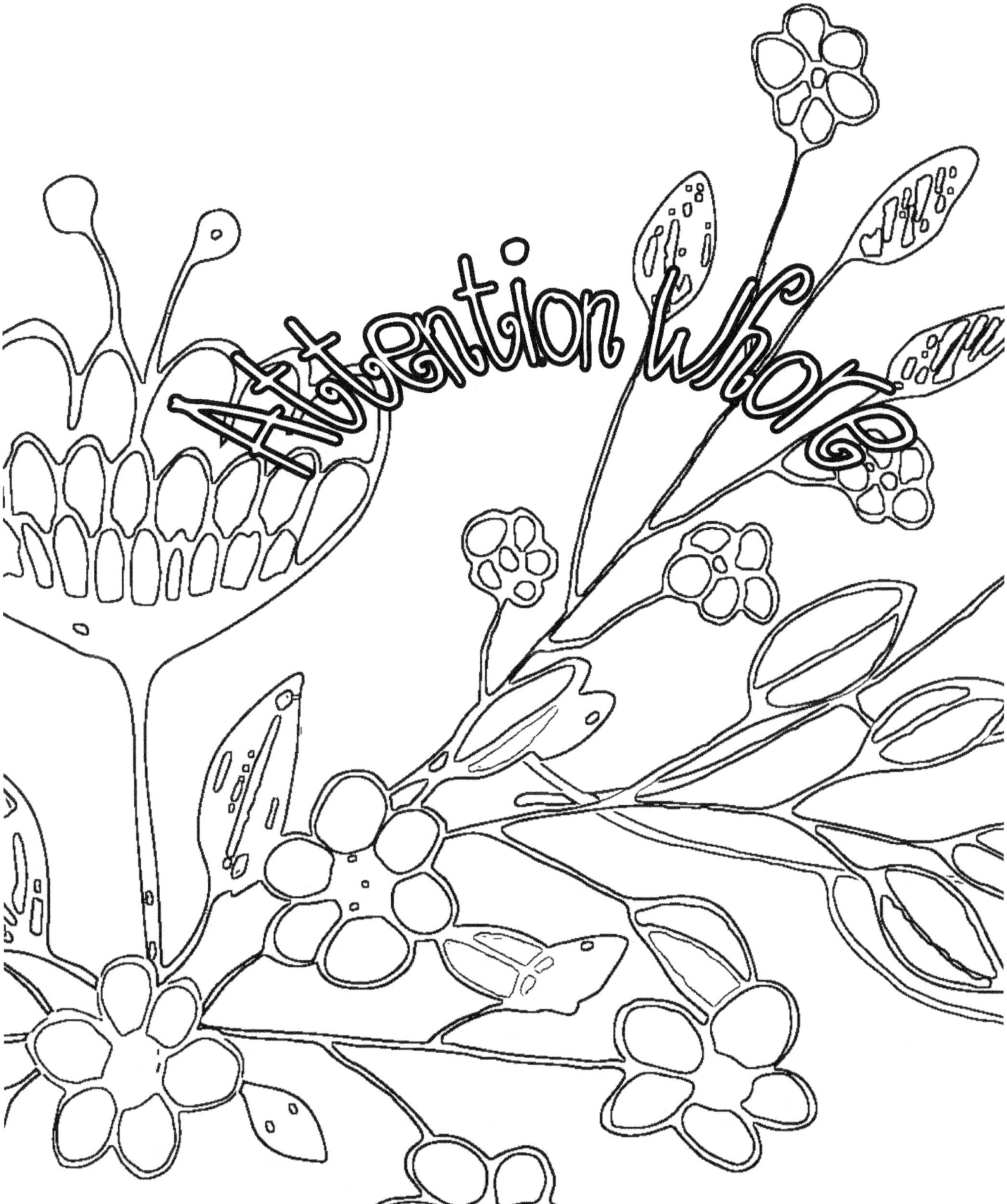
Attention Whore

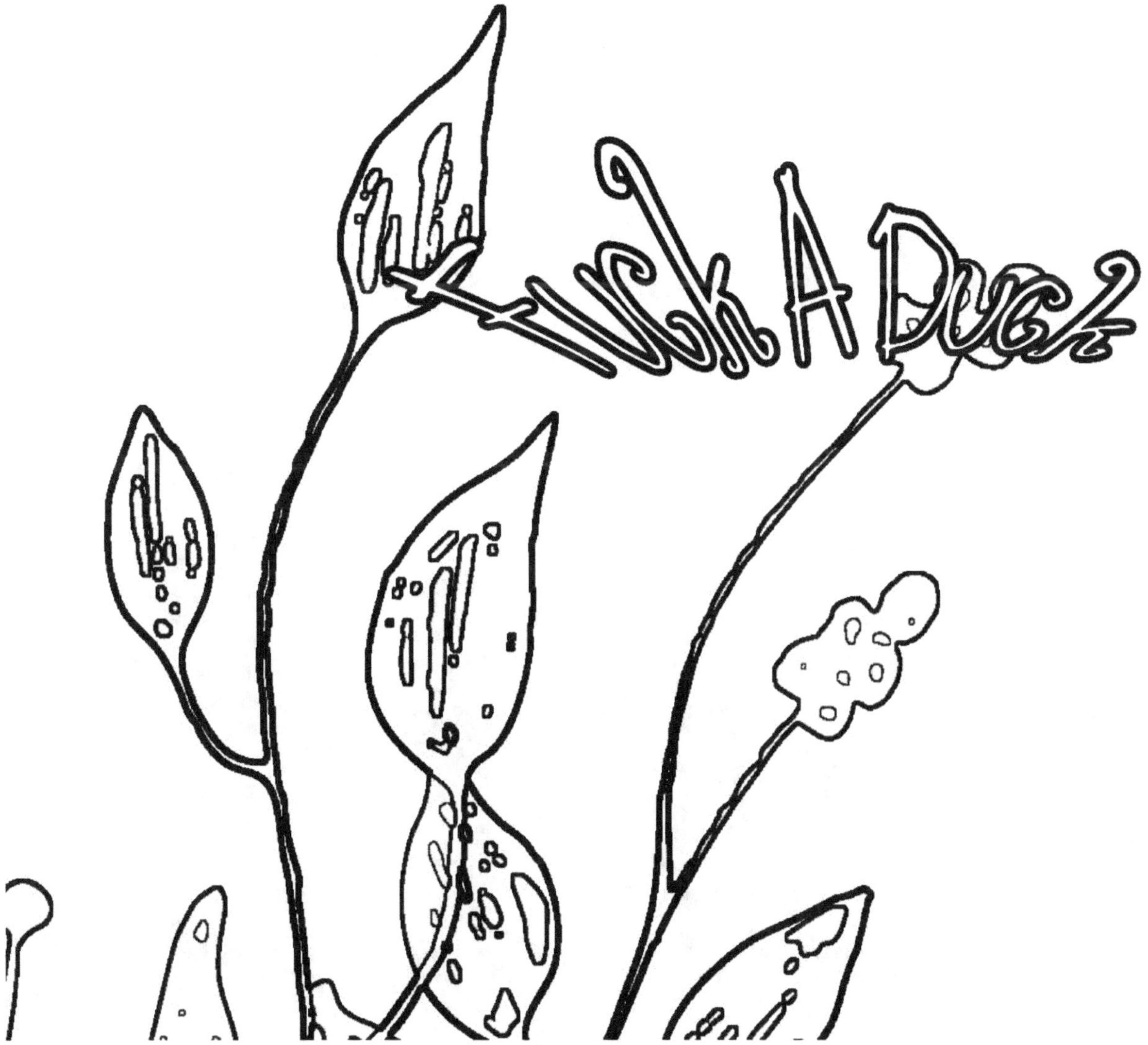
Fuck A Duck

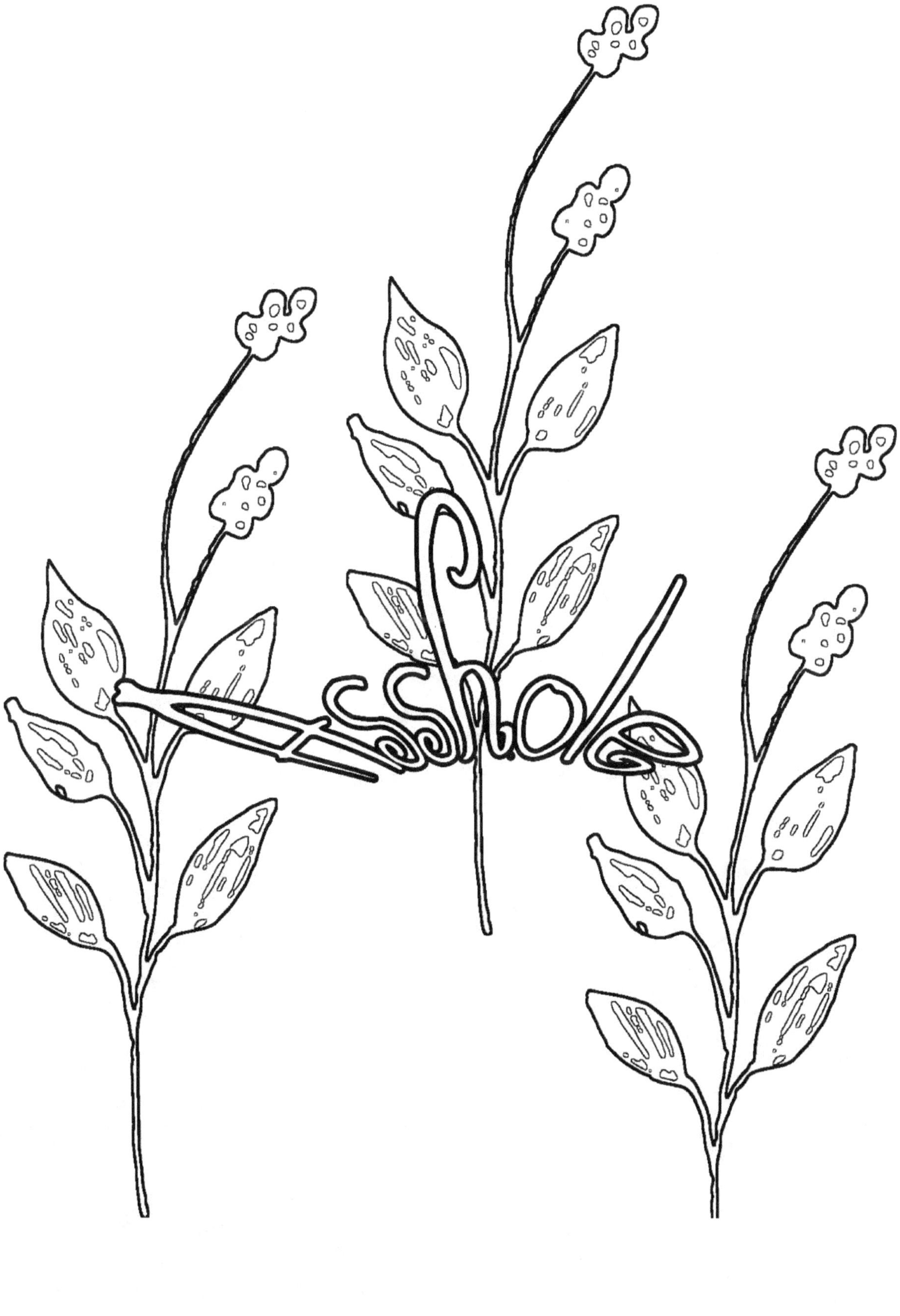
Asshole

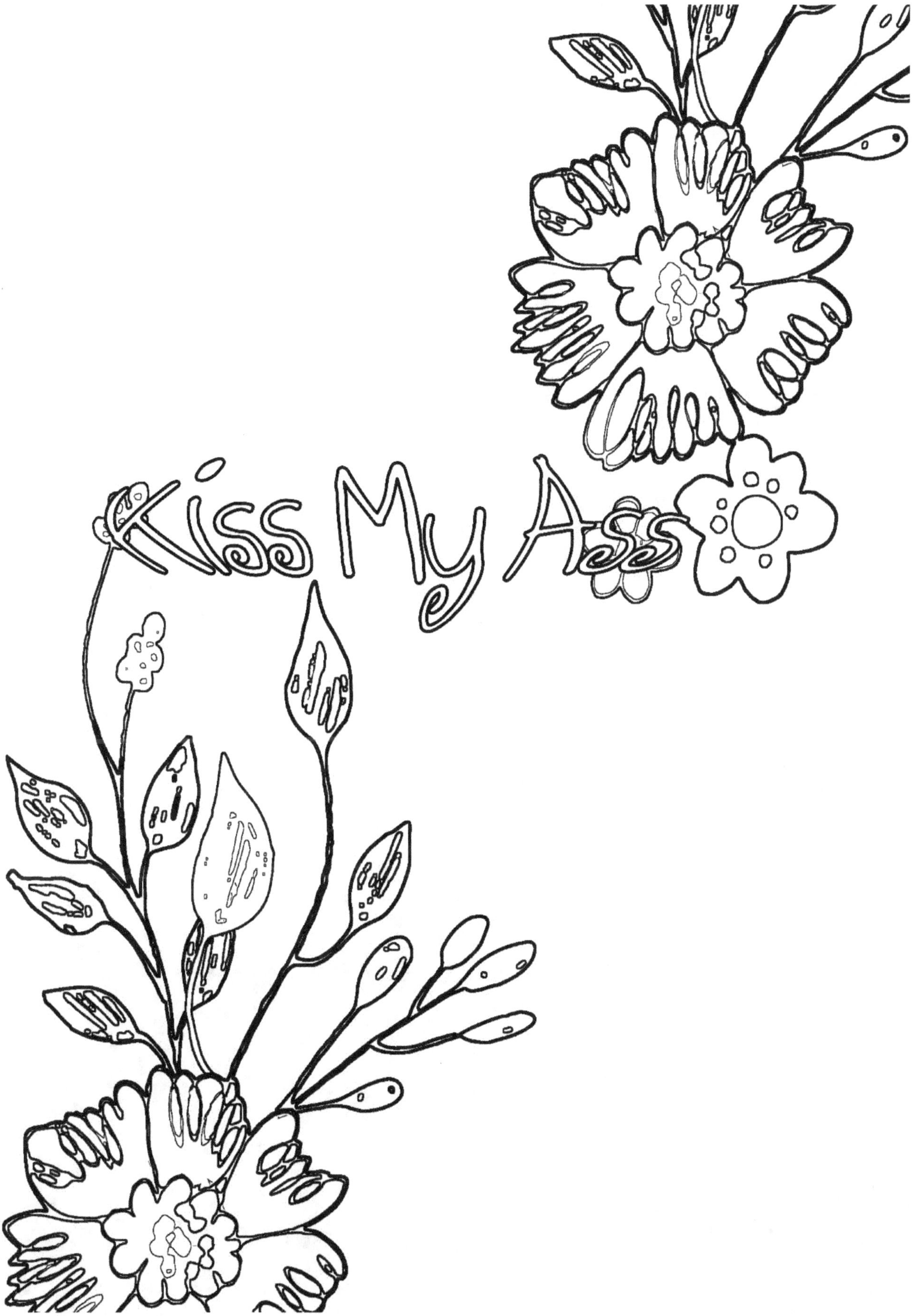
Kiss My Ass

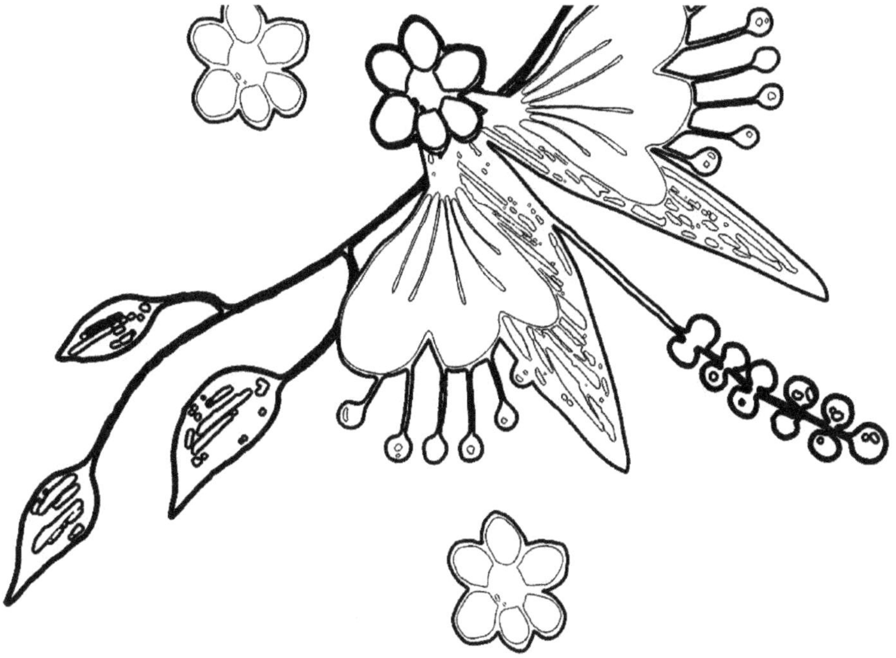

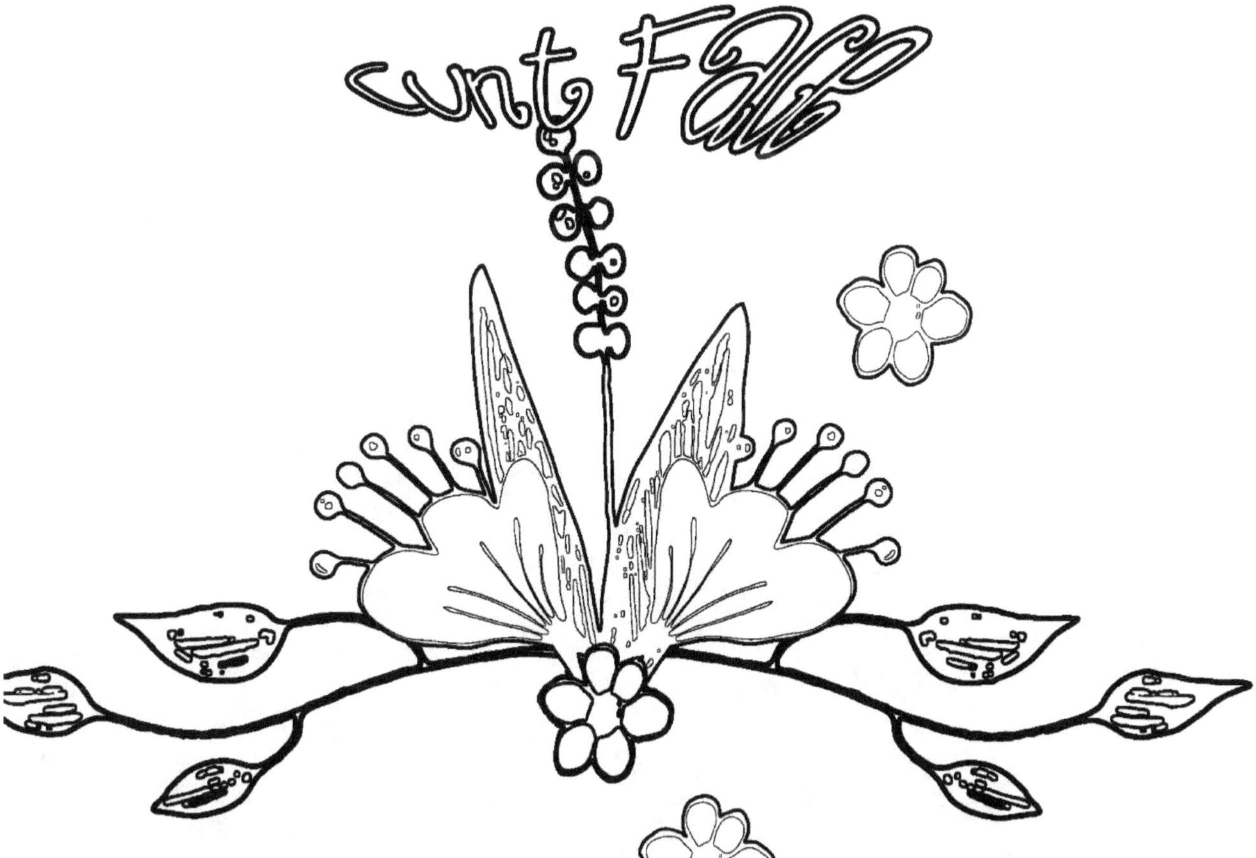
cunt

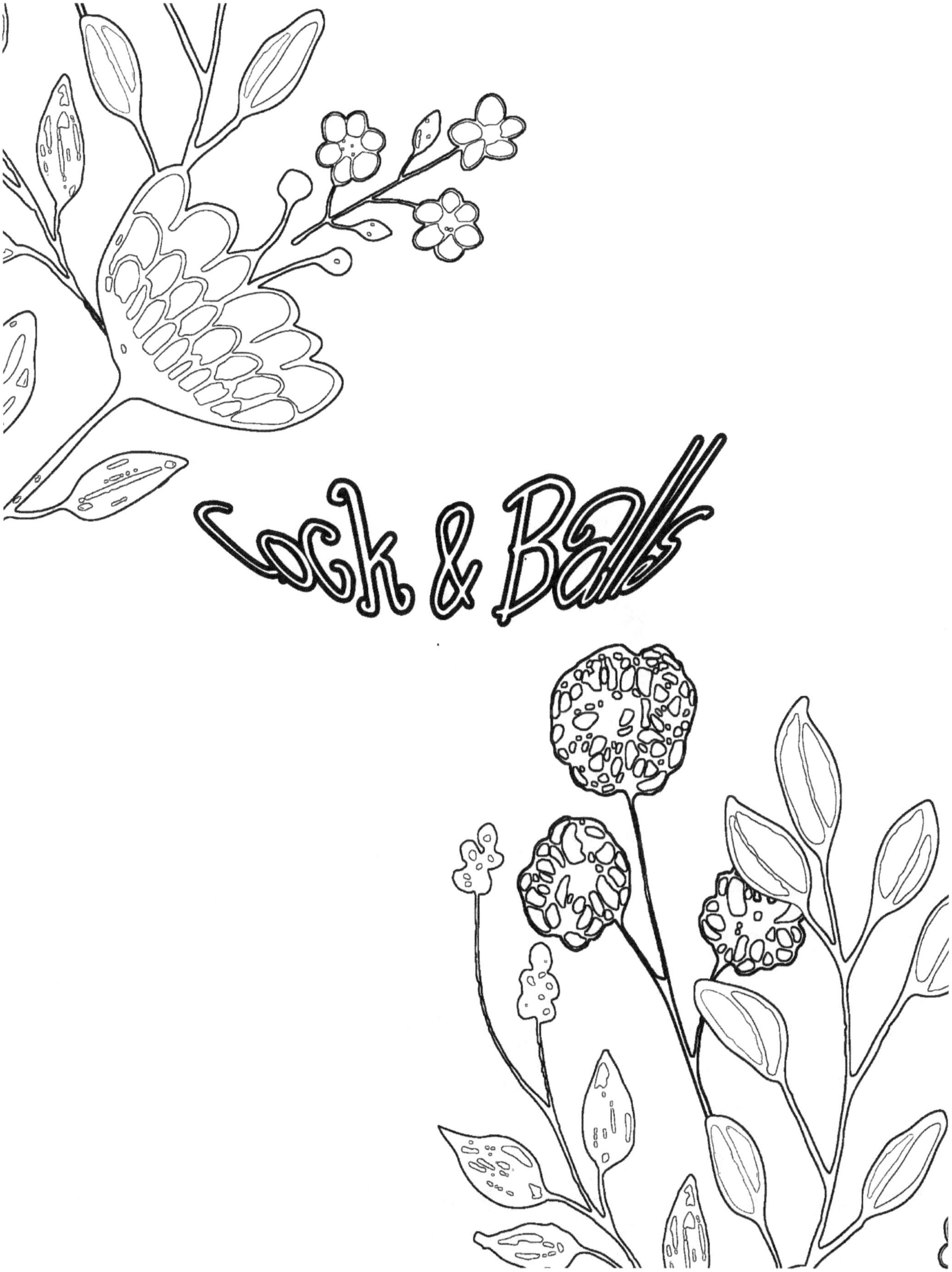
Cock & Balls

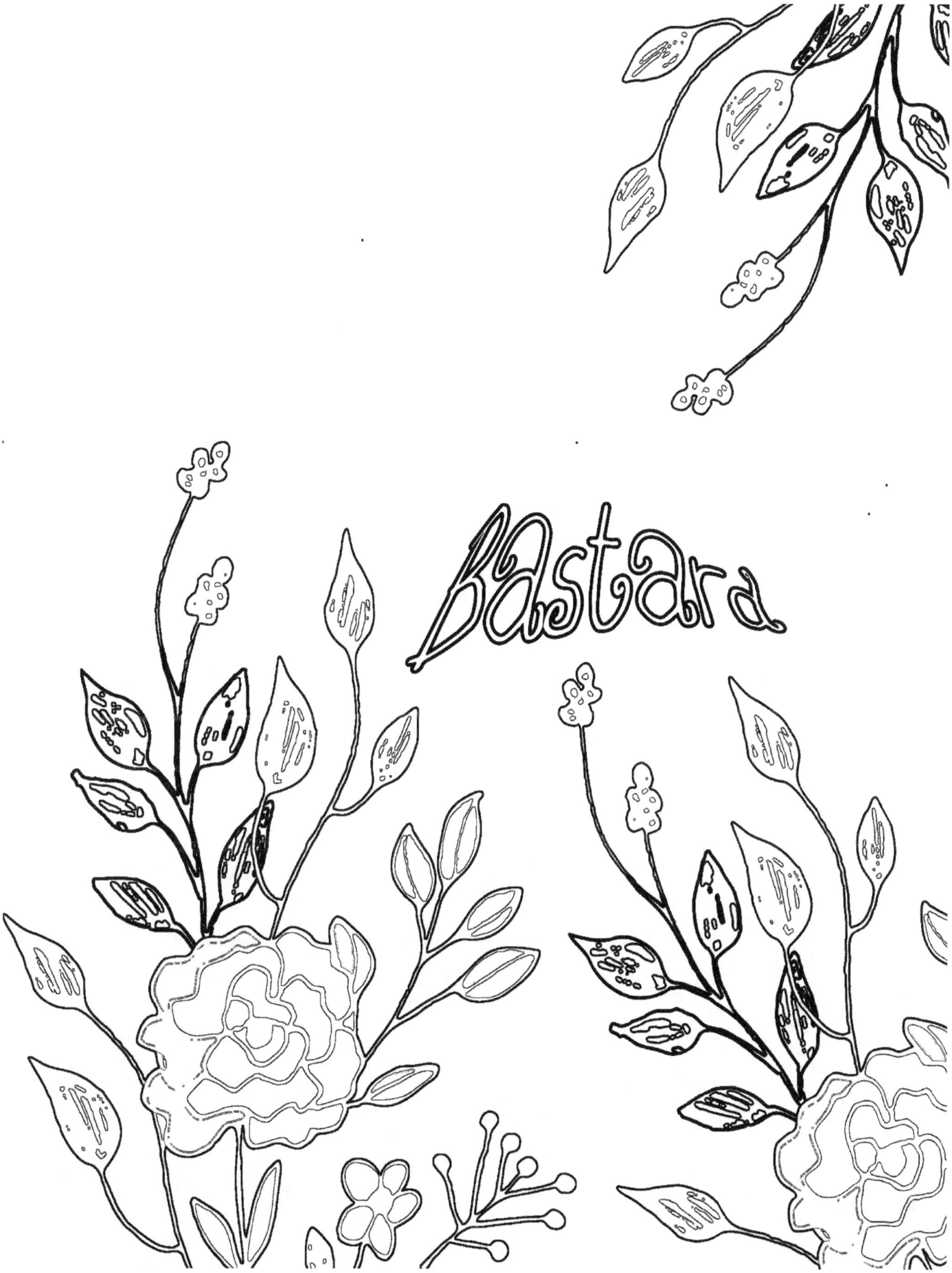
Bastara

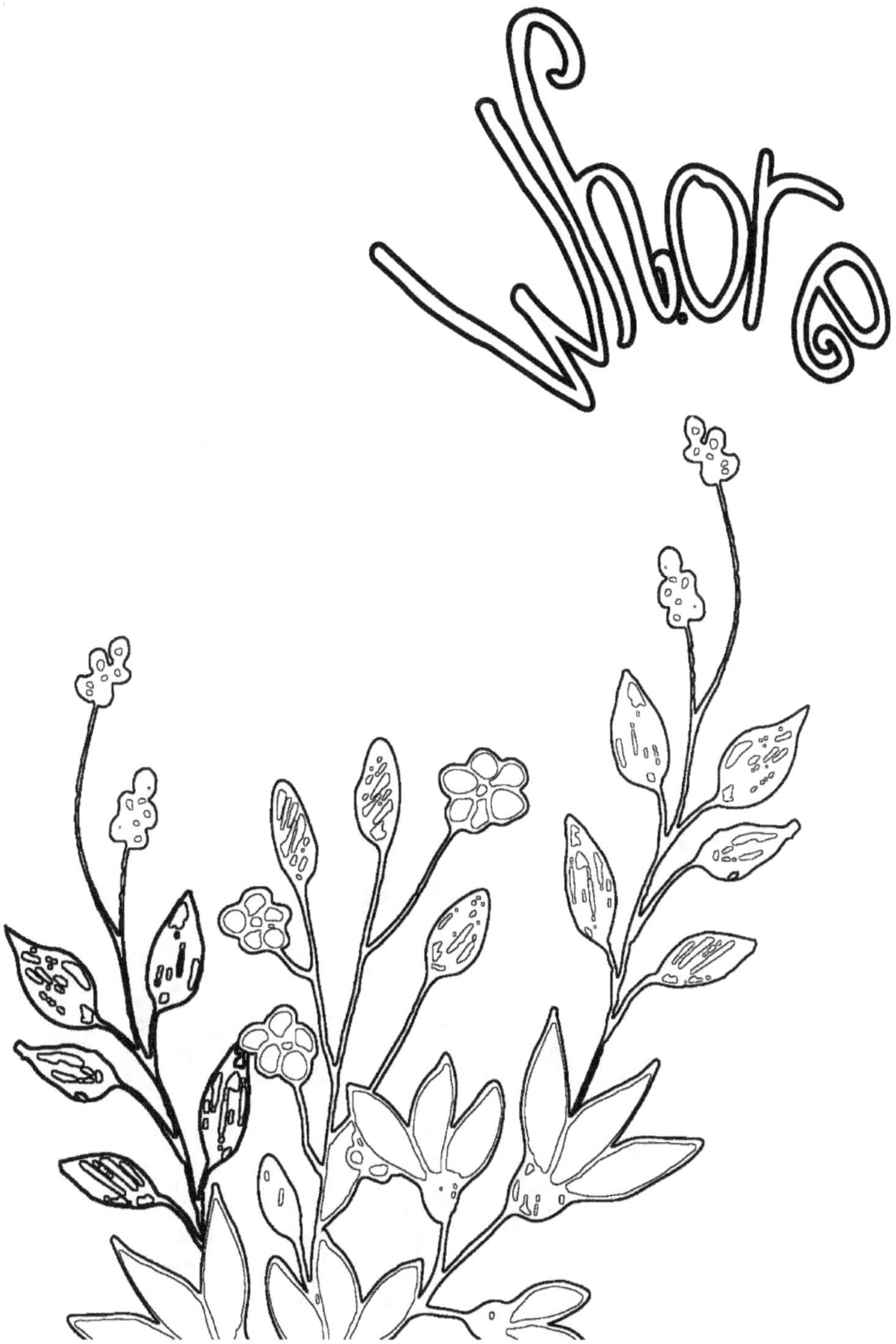
Whore

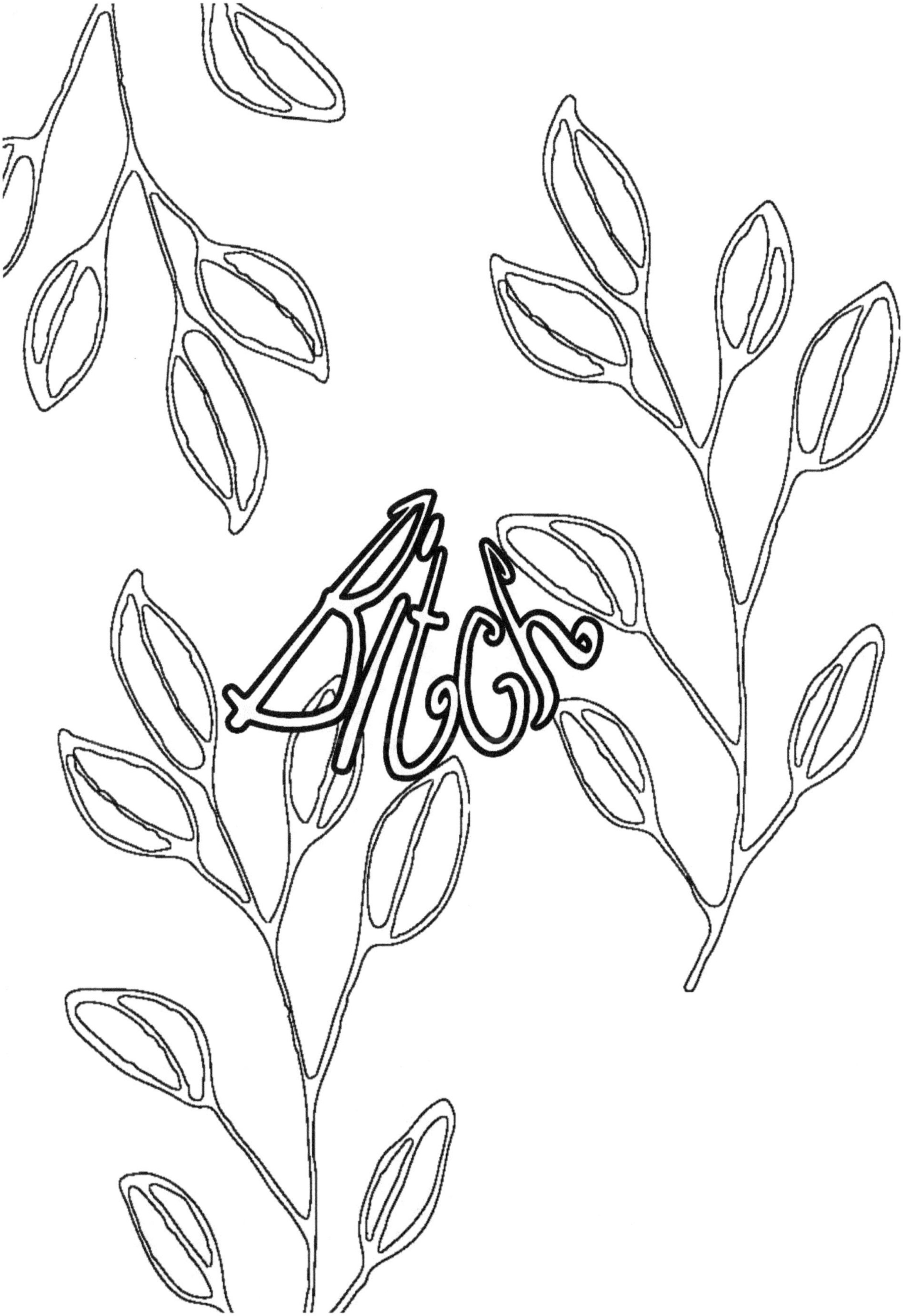
Bitch

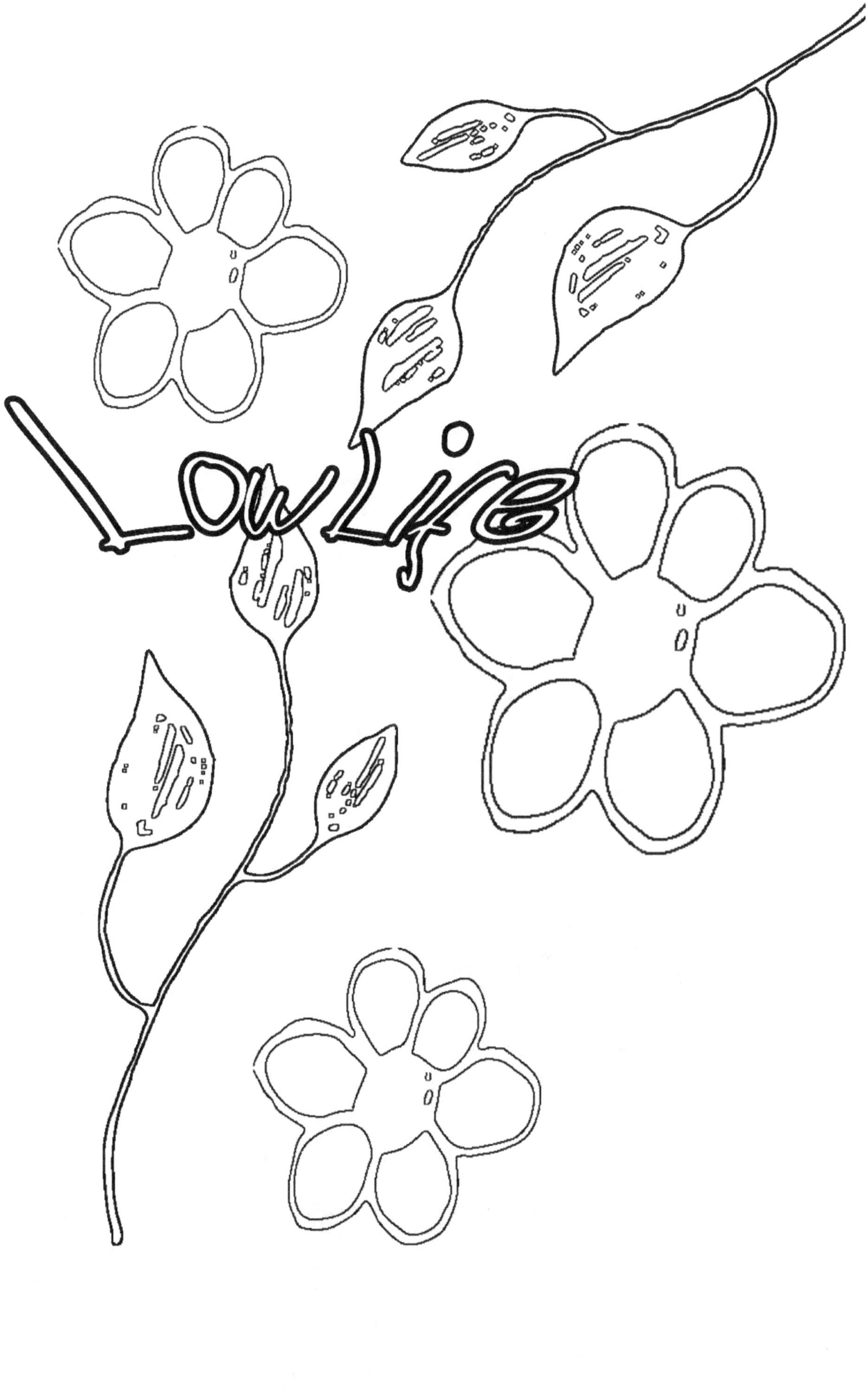
Low Life

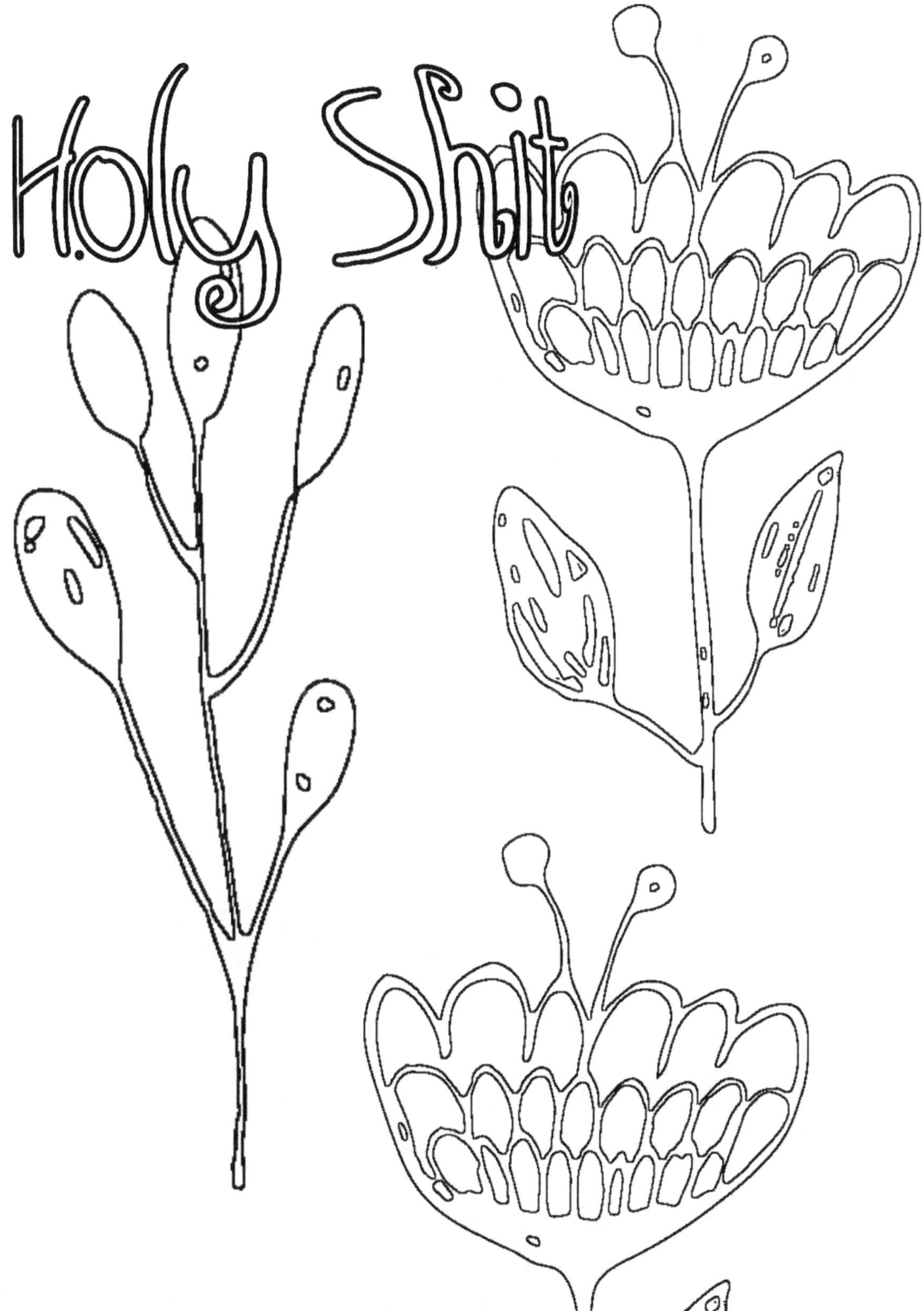
Holy Shit

www.ingramcontent.com/pod-product-compliance
Lightning Source LLC
Chambersburg PA
CBHW081751170526
45167CB00009B/3996
* 9 7 8 1 5 4 2 8 1 0 1 6 6 *